Secret Worlds

Too Slow To See

Kim Taylor

Delacorte
Press

Published by Delacorte Press
Bantam Doubleday Dell Publishing Group, Inc.
666 Fifth Avenue, New York, New York 10103
This edition was first published in Great Britain
in 1989 by Belitha Press Limited.
Text copyright © Kim Taylor 1989
Photographs copyright © Kim Taylor and
Jane Burton 1989
Consultant: S. Patricia Manning

Manufactured in Italy for Imago Publishing
May 1991
10 9 8 7 6 5 4 3 2 1

**Library of Congress Cataloging in Publication
Data**

Taylor, Kim.
  Too slow to see/Kim Taylor.
    p. cm.—(Secret worlds)
  ISBN 0-385-30214-2
  ISBN 0-385-30215-0 (lib. bdg.)
  1. Motion perception (Vision)—Juvenile
literature. 2. Growth—Juvenile literature.
  3. Change—Juvenile literature.
I. Title. II. Series: Taylor, Kim. Secret worlds.
BF245.T39 1991
508—dc20   90-3337
                                                  CIP
                                                  AC

*I*F YOU WATCH CAREFULLY, YOU CAN SEE A SNAIL CREEP along, but can you see a plant grow or an ice crystal form? Some things in nature happen so slowly that you need a long memory to be sure that anything has happened at all. Frost is ice formed from water in the air. It grows slowly during the night, when the air is damp, forming beautiful patterns on windows and leaves.

Icicles, too, can grow overnight, but if you sit down to watch one grow, you soon get bored as well as cold. As each drop forms at the tip of the icicle, it slowly freezes, and the icicle grows straight downward. The icicles below are curved because the twig supporting them is being bent gradually by the growing weight of ice.

Turned to stone

*A*N ICICLE CAN GROW IN ONE NIGHT, A PLANT MAY TAKE a year to grow, while a tree can take hundreds of years. All these things happen quickly compared with the time it takes a fossil to form. A fossil is a plant or animal that has lain in the ground for so long it has been turned to stone. It takes at least a million years for a fossil to form. The fossil leaf (*above left*) is of a ginkgo tree that lived 150 million years ago. Amazingly, there are still ginkgo trees alive now (*above right*), and their leaves look just the same.

When a fish dies, its body sinks to the bottom of the sea. As it lies there, its flesh is eaten by small creatures or rots away, leaving a perfect skeleton. Layers of mud gradually cover the skeleton, pressing it flat.

Very slowly an extraordinary change takes place. The soft mud hardens into rock, and the bones of the skeleton themselves turn to stone. Millions of years later the rock is split open, and there, pressed flat between layers of stone, is the fossil skeleton of the fish that died fifty million years ago (*below left*). Today similar fish are swimming in the sea (*below right*), but their bones will not become fossils until millions of years into the future.

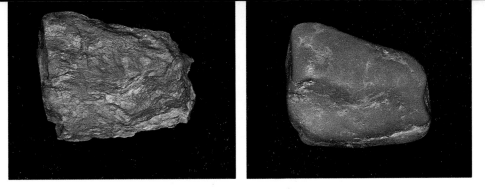

Every pebble on the beach . . .

OCEAN WAVES POUND ONTO A BEACH OF PEBBLES (*opposite*). The pebbles are smooth and rounded, and they are made of different sorts of rocks. Where did they come from and how did they form? Most pebbles start out as rough chips of rock (*above left*). As the waves rattle the chips together, their roughness is ground away (*above right*). You can hear the grinding of the pebbles if you stand on a shingle (pebble) beach on a rough day. It does not take more than a few weeks for a pebble to form (*below*). You can even find pieces of broken bottles that have been worn into pebbles. If pebbles are always getting smaller, where do the bits that are ground away go? The answer is simple: They drift away to form beaches of fine sand.

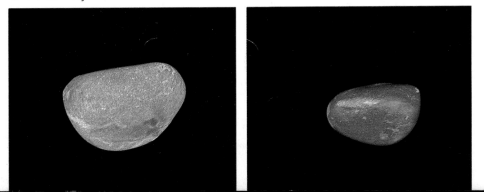

From kitten to cat

WHEN A KITTEN IS BORN, ITS EYES ARE CLOSED, AND IT is only just able to crawl (*above left*). All it wants is to be kept warm and to suckle milk from its mother. Milk is a rich food, and the kitten grows, but growth is too slow for you to see it happening. Even if you look at the kitten only once a day, it is difficult to see the changes. But if you wait for two weeks, the changes are very easy to see (*above right*). The kitten is now much bigger, and its eyes are open wide.

After five weeks the kitten is a small cat (*above left*). Its ears and teeth have grown, and it is able to pounce and play. Growing up happens slowly because it is very complicated. The food that the kitten eats has to be digested and used to build its body and to give it energy. Learning is another important part of growing up that also takes time. The kitten has to learn how to walk, run, climb, and jump. When you see kittens playing together, they are learning all the time so that when they become full-grown cats (*above right*), they can do everything a cat needs to do.

9

A new beginning

P LANTS CAN GROW MUCH MORE QUICKLY THAN ANIMALS, but their growth is still too slow for you to see it happening. In early spring some plants like this aconite (*opposite*) seem to burst out of the ground. This one was photographed each day for six days. You can count the days.

A wood anemone bursts out of the ground in spring. It can do this because it has food stored in its roots. The shoot comes out of the ground like a hairpin (above left). In three days it has straightened (*above right*). After five days the flower bud is visible (*below left*). On day eleven (*below right*) the flower is fully open and ready for bees to visit.

11

Opening time

A BUD IS LIKE A PACKAGE: IT HAS A WRAPPING INSIDE which something has been carefully packed. This hibiscus bud (*below left*) is tightly packed. If you squeeze it gently, you can feel that it is quite hard. Come back the next day, and the bud has burst into five sepals with crumpled pink petals peeping out (*below right*).

All the time the hibiscus petals are expanding and pushing farther out of the bud, but the movement is too slow to see. By the next day the petals are half out of the bud (*below left*). And in another day the flower is fully open (*below right*). Flowers are able to open quickly because they are simply expanding, not growing. All the growing has already happened, during the many months that the buds took to form.

Spring action

WHITE BRYONY IS A CLIMBING PLANT. IT CANNOT STAND UP ON its own, so it clings to other plants or even trees. It holds on with tendrils—special branches that wind around other plants. Bryony tendrils form into springs so that the plant is held gently when the wind blows. The tendril first emerges as a coil (*above*) which in a day straightens out and winds around whatever it touches (*below left*). A day later the straight tendril starts to kink (*below right*) and in another day it has formed a perfect spring (*opposite*).

Slowly, slowly . . . catch your dinner

*T*HE CAPE SUNDEW LIVES IN BOGGY PLACES WHERE THE soil is very poor. It needs more to live on than the soil can provide, so it catches insects and eats them. Its leaves are covered with red hairs, each tipped with a tiny sticky blob. When a fly settles on a leaf, its legs stick to the blobs, and it cannot escape (*above left*). The sundew leaf then starts to bend (*above right*).

Gradually the leaf curls around the fly until it is bent double (*above left and right*). Now the process of digestion begins. The leaf oozes a special juice that dissolves the insides of the fly. The juice is then soaked up again by the leaf and helps make the plant grow. All that is left of the fly is its skeleton, which you can sometimes see on sundew leaves when they straighten out again to wait for another meal.

Chasing the sun

MANY FLOWERS, LIKE THESE LESSER CELANDINES, open in the morning and then shut up at night. They do this because they need to attract bees, and bees fly only in the daytime. You can imagine flowers as being like shops: They open in the morning for their customers, the bees, which come to collect nectar, bringing a few grains of pollen from another flower in exchange. Some flowers give out scent to attract bees; the warmer they are, the more scent they have. You can't see it happening, but celandines actually follow the sun as it moves overhead (*opposite*) so that they can trap its warmth all day.

A stinking feast

NOT ALL THE ACTION IS HAPPENING IN THE DAYTIME. As the sun sets (*below*), the egg-shaped young stinkhorns begin to develop under the leaf litter in the woods. They are not really eggs but are egg-sized and whitish. As darkness falls, the top of the "egg" splits, and within four hours the stinkhorn has fully risen (*opposite*). By morning it starts to stink. You can smell it from yards away, and so can hungry flies, which rush to feast on its smelly slime covering the spore-bearing crown. When they leave, they carry stinkhorn spores with them on their feet to "plant" at their next landing places.

The sun goes down

*A*LL DAY LONG THE SUN MOVES ACROSS THE SKY, BUT the only time you can see it move is when it rises or sets, and even then it creeps so slowly you can barely detect any movement. From the first peep of the sun above the horizon until its full round shape is in the sky takes just about three minutes. The picture opposite shows the sun going down again. It has been photographed every six minutes as it sets. It goes straight down at an angle to the horizon. If you lived on the equator, you would see the sun go straight down. After the sun has set, the sky glows with beautiful colors.

23

The spinning earth

NOT ONLY DOES THE SUN MOVE, BUT THE STARS MOVE as well. In fact, everything in the sky appears to move because the Earth, with you on it, is spinning around. Here you can see how the Earth spins when a camera looks toward the polestar for one and a half hours on a clear and frosty night. As the Earth turns, the polestar appears to be a bright blob, and each star leaves a curved streak on the film in the stationary camera. The stars themselves glitter blue, white, yellow, or reddish in the deep night sky.